98th U.S. Open Championship
The Olympic Club
June 18-21, 1998

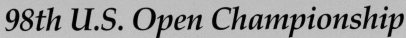

Par and Yardage

Hole	Par	Yardage	Hole	Par	Yardage
1	5	533	10	4	422
2	4	394	11	4	430
3	3	223	12	4	416
4	4	438	13	3	186
5	4	457	14	4	422
6	4	437	15	3	157
7	4	288	16	5	609
8	3	137	17	4	468
9	4	433	18	4	347
	35	3,340		35	3,457
				70	6,797

98th
U.S. Open
The Olympic Club

Writer
Robert Sommers

Photographers
Michael Cohen
Fred Vuich

Editor
Bev Norwood

ISBN 1-878843-22-2

©1998 United States Golf Association®
Golf House, Far Hills, N.J. 07931

Statistics produced by Unisys Corporation

Course illustration by Dan Wardlaw © The Major Series Magazine

Published by International Merchandising Corporation,
1360 East Ninth Street, Cleveland, Ohio 44114

Designed and produced by Davis Design

Printed in the United States of America

98th U.S. Open

Official Annual Presented by

ROLEX

Once again, Lee Janzen has shown that he thrives on major championships. I was impressed with Lee's attitude and approach to the game as well as his shotmaking ability even before he won his first Open in 1993 at Baltusrol. He is a particularly strong player under the stress that goes along with major championships, and has shown that on a number of occasions since Baltusrol.

That certainly was the case at The Olympic Club, especially on the last few holes Sunday afternoon, when the pressure always mounts on the contenders. The golf course is one that, in a way, played to Janzen's strong points. Olympic is a tenacious course. It is vitally important to drive the ball in the fairway and keep it there. Because of the speed of the greens, the players had to have the ability to keep their putting under control all of the time. Again, the golf course and Janzen went hand-in-hand in producing the rewarding results for him.

It is a pleasure to introduce this 14th annual commemorative book on the U.S. Open for our friends at Rolex Watch USA. I'm sure that its readers will enjoy this in-depth story of the 1998 championship and the outstanding photographs. As always, the United States Golf Association will devote all proceeds from the sale of the book for use in connection with its junior golf activities.

Arnold Palmer

In the days immediately after the gold strike at Sutter's Mill, in 1848, San Francisco claimed a population of seven people. The other 813 had fled to the gold fields, about 100 miles to the northeast. Even before James F. Marshall found the first few gleaming nuggets near John Sutter's sawmill, the city had been somewhat less than a metropolis. It had 200 houses, two wharfs, two hotels and one newspaper, the *Star*, a small publication owned by Sam Brannen.

Brannen led the rush to the fields. Within days, San Francisco had nearly disappeared.

Soon, though, a city began taking shape. Blessed with one of the world's great harbors, it became the staging point for the 'Forty-Niners, the men, and the occasional woman, from around the world who arrived via the Pacific Ocean dreaming of instant wealth. As gold-hungry as their passengers, the crews joined the frenzy, leaving their ships to rot in the great bay.

With all its hysteria, the Gold Rush eventually created the great city. Within the next two years, California became the nation's 31st state and San Francisco a vibrant community. The population swelled, and a collection of tents and shacks grew into a permanent metropolis.

Fortunes made in the gold fields brought culture to San Francisco. Overnight millionaires built lavish houses, theaters opened, bringing leading actors, singers and opera stars to town, and debating societies formed.

Younger elements in the flourishing city looked for other outlets as well. In 1860, a year before the Civil War broke out, a group of young athletes met regularly at the home

The 18th hole, par 4 and 347 yards.

of Charles and Arthur Nahl and worked out in the Nahls' backyard. Soon one of them suggested they form a club. They called it The Olympic Club, even though the Olympic Games hadn't been played in nearly 1,500 years.

Like the city, The Olympic Club thrived. It started in a fire house, moved several times, and in 1912 settled into a five-story building near Union Square, one of the city's landmarks. Its facilities included a gymnasium with a track, squash and handball courts, a billiard room and a Turkish bath.

Olympic members competed in baseball, basketball, billiards, bowling, boxing, crew, cricket, cycling, fencing, football, golf, gymnastics, handball, ice hockey, pistol and rifle shooting, polo, rugby, soccer, squash, swimming and diving, tennis, track and field, volleyball, water polo and wrestling.

The club attracted superb athletes from the beginning. In its finest hour, Olympic sent 22 of its members to the 1924 Olympic Games in Paris, more than any other organization. Earlier, a Wells Fargo Bank clerk, James J. Corbett, had taught boxing at the club, then turned professional, and in 1892 knocked out John L. Sullivan for the world heavyweight championship.

In track and field, Cornelius Warmerdam, the first man to pole vault over 15 feet, raised the record to 15 feet 1⅛ inches in 1940, and two years later raised it again to 15 feet 7¾ inches; Parry O'Brian put the shot 60 feet 8½ inches and Lon Spurner ran the 880 in 1:47, a world's record, in 1955; in 1941, Grover Klemmer ran the 400 meters in 46 seconds, another world's record.

In tennis, Olympians Maurice McLoughlin won the national championship in 1912 and 1913, and William M. (Little Bill) Johnston in 1915 and 1919 and Wimbledon in 1923.

Olympic ran up an equally strong record in team sports. Led by Hank Luisetti, who had pioneered the one-hand shot at Stanford, its basketball team took second place in the 1941 AAU Championships.

Made up of former college stars, its football team played nearby colleges like Stanford, California, Santa Clara, St. Mary's and the University of San Francisco. Its 1925 team was undefeated, but with the rise of the National Football League, its supply of college players dried up, and Olympic played its last season in 1932.

Golf has been part of the Olympic program since after the First World War, when the Lakeside Golf and Country Club offered to rent its course to The Olympic Club for nothing more than the cost of maintenance. The members took to the game as they had to everything else they tried. Olympic is said to have more low-handicap golfers than any other club in the West, and two of its members won the U.S. Open and another the PGA Championship. Bob Rosburg, a former Stanford athlete, won the 1959

PGA, Ken Venturi won the 1964 Open, and in the 1966 Open at Olympic, 19-year-old amateur Johnny Miller shot 290, tied for eighth place, a higher finish than Mark Kuchar in 1998, and beat Ben Hogan by one stroke.

In 1922, Olympic bought out Lakeside and its 365 acres for less than $500,000.

Lakeside sat on prime property, situated on high bluffs overlooking the Pacific Ocean where, on a clear day, the Golden Gate, the entrance to the magnificent harbor, sparkled in the sunlight. The air was fresh and clear and the Pacific moisture and cool climate encouraged the grass golf courses needed.

After Olympic took over, the club decided to abandon the original course and build two others, the Ocean Course, which ranged along the cliffs overlooking the Pacific, and the Lake Course, which approaches but doesn't border Lake Merced.

A landslide wiped out a big chunk of the Ocean Course in 1926 and the entire concept had to be re-worked. Sam Whiting, an Englishman who had worked on the original project with Willie Wilson, a Scotsman, re-designed both courses.

The Ocean Course was fun and more

The third hole, par 3 and 223 yards.

The eighth hole, par 3 and 137 yards.

scenic; the Lake Course has always been the more testing. Two of the most remembered U.S. Opens have been played there. In the first, in 1955, Hogan believed he had won his fifth Open when he turned in a score of 287, but Jack Fleck, an obscure player living in Davenport, Iowa, tied him and then beat him in a playoff the next day. Eleven years later, Arnold Palmer went into the last nine holes leading Billy Casper, in second place, by seven strokes. Casper shot 32, Palmer 39, and Casper won the playoff the next day.

With a wonderful burst of scoring, Scott Simpson birdied three of the last six holes and won the 1987 Open by one stroke over Tom Watson, and Lee Janzen made up six strokes on Payne Stewart in the last round and won the 1998 championship.

In those four Opens, and in the 1958 and 1981 U.S. Amateur Championships, Olympic has stood up to the best golfers in the game. The winning Open scores there have ranged from the 287s of Fleck and Hogan to the 277 of Simpson. Casper and Palmer tied with 278, and Janzen shot 280, even par.

Built along the sides of hills, Olympic isn't long, a few yards short of 6,800 yards (Congressional Country Club measured 7,213 yards for the 1997 Open), but because of the hilly ground and some other characteristics, length doesn't seem to matter. One of its par 4s, the seventh, measures less than 300 yards, and the closing hole, at 347 yards, ranks among the shortest closing holes in championship golf. Two other holes, though, are exceptionally long. The 16th, a man-sized par 5, stretches 609 yards, and the hybrid 17th reaches 468 yards.

Olympic's difficulties lie in its other features. The land had been barren when it bought out Lakeside, but in one of its first acts the club planted 40,000 trees — eucalyptus, cypress, Monterey pines and California redwoods. They leave every fairway a narrow avenue bordered by fierce rough and towering trees that intimidate the careful player as well as the free swinger. The Lake Course's strengths lie in those tight fairways, dense, unyielding rough and in its small, hard, slick and sloping greens

Some of those fairways are unusually difficult to hold. For example, the second,

The ninth hole, par 4 and 433 yards.

fourth, fifth and ninth turn in one direction, but the ground cants in the other. Take the fourth, a 438-yard par 4 played from a high hill into a valley and then back up again to the green. The fairway bends from right to left, but the fairway slants to the right. The drive commonly hits the side of the hill and rolls across the fairway toward the rough.

This, along with the fifth and the ninth, which bend left to right, were the most difficult fairways to hit. A fraction over 38 percent of the drives held their fairways. The fourth also ranked as the second most difficult green to hold. With a practically blind second shot to the green set on a high rise, only 23 percent held the green.

This wasn't the worst. The 17th held only 13 percent.

The 17th has been a controversial hole in the last two Olympic Opens. A par 5 for members, it measures a little over 500 yards

for club play, but in setting up the course for the Open, the United States Golf Association has routinely used shorter tees and proclaimed it a par 4, but at varying lengths. It measured 461 yards in 1955, 443 in 1966, 428 in 1987 and 468 in 1998.

Its fairway runs along a hillside, the ground rises beyond the drive zone to a small green built to accept a high pitch rather than a long iron, and it is ringed with deep and fluffy bunkers. Some players griped that this was not a proper par-4 hole, that they occasionally had to play a wooden club for their second shots. Before the championship began, Tom Lehman, one of the favorites, confessed he had hit his 3-wood for his second shot in each of his practice rounds. Tom Watson reached it with a 2-iron.

Nevertheless, there was reason behind the conversion. Olympic's normal configuration ends with a 609-yard par 5, a 505-

yard par 5 and a 347-yard par 4 — all wedge shots into the green. An Open shouldn't end this way. Therefore, the green of the 17th has traditionally been brought within range of the second shot and called a par 4.

Changing the number completely changes the players' attitudes. Where they might be tempted to lay up and avoid the risk of playing a fairway wood or long iron to the tight opening into the green if the hole had been labeled a par 5, as a par 4, they feel they must take the dare and play a forcing shot, a shot that makes the player reach, makes him extend himself while at the same time possibly exposing a weakness.

There are some who believe every Open should ask for a dangerous shot on its closing holes. Certainly the 17th at Congressional, with its green jutting into a lake,

asked as much as the 17th at Olympic. As Ernie Els, Colin Montgomerie and Tom Lehman came down that hill, all three men needed birdies. Only Els played the shot he had to play, birdied and won the championship.

As Janzen reached Olympic's 17th, he had one stroke in hand and couldn't afford to play safely; he had to go for the green. He couldn't have played the hole better. After a terrific drive to just the right spot on the fairway, he threaded a nerveless 3-iron through the narrow gap onto the back of the green and made his par. Minutes later Stewart made his par, but the game had changed by then; he needed more.

Holes like this, and indeed courses like this — harsh and demanding — make the United States Open the game's premier championship.

The 17th hole, par 4 and 468 yards.

Even though the courts struck down the PGA Tour's ban against players riding golf carts, the issue wouldn't fade away. It was the subject of a widely covered and lengthy press conference two days before the opening shots of the 1998 U.S. Open.

The issue of riding a cart was brought to court by Casey Martin, a 26-year-old former Stanford golfer who has been stricken with Klippel-Trenauney-Webber Syndrome, a painful, incurable disease that afflicts the circulatory system of his right leg. It has caused his muscles to atrophy and bones to deteriorate.

After hearing from lawyers representing both the PGA Tour and Martin, Magistrate Judge Thomas M. Coffin, of the United States District Court of the District of Oregon, issued an injunction against the PGA Tour's banning carts for Martin. Judge Coffin deliberated the issue no more than three hours.

Citing the Americans With Disabilities Act, Martin's lawyers brought the suit because Martin wanted to play golf professionally, even though he felt he couldn't walk 18 holes, the usual requirement for championship golf. Judge Coffin, described once as "not a country club guy," obviously didn't agree.

Everyone does agree, though, that Martin is a first-class golfer. Before the temporary injunction became permanent, he won a tournament on the Nike Tour, and then he qualified for the U.S. Open and played so exceptionally well he shot 291 and tied for 23rd place, 11 strokes behind Lee Janzen. A strong driver, he averaged 291 yards on

Despite the media and gallery attention, Casey Martin performed well and tied for 23rd.

selected holes, second only to John Daly's 295-yard average.

Judge Coffin delivered a very narrow decision. It related only to Martin and only against the PGA Tour. Evidently not bound by the decision, since the U.S. Open is conducted by the United States Golf Association, not the PGA Tour, the USGA nevertheless allowed Martin to ride in both the sectional qualifying round and the Open proper.

The judge's decision and Martin's Nike Tour victory made him a celebrity. When he qualified in the sectional round in Cincinnati, about 60 reporters from around the country turned up at the Clovernook Country Club. The *Los Angeles Times* sent Thomas Bonk, the newspaper's golf writer, and the *New York Times* sent Clifton Brown, its golf writer. The *Los Angeles Times* gave Martin's qualifying top billing on its sports page, topped by a page-wide 72-point banner headline, "Martin Gets Ticket to Ride." Bonk's article ran 25½ column inches, and two pictures another 24½, making 50 inches for a qualifying round more than 2,000 miles from home.

Coverage of this sort indicated how important the press perceived the issue.

Further evidence arrived at 2 o'clock Tuesday afternoon of Open week when Martin arrived at the press center for his press conference. The interview room was jammed with reporters, columnists, television personalities and anyone else who could shoulder his way in. The room held 250 seats. Every chair was taken, and 50 or more standees crowded the rear of the room. Eleven television cameras recorded the session, and ESPN, The Golf Channel and one local station broadcast the interview live. While the session didn't run as long as Tiger Woods' 45-minute interview a year earlier, it lasted about half an hour.

A condensed sampling of questions and responses:

• Does his leg cause him pain all the time?

It constantly pains him when he walks over a period of time, but the pain has definitely been reduced because he rides.

• On the reaction of other players to his playing.

Without exception everyone has been extremely kind and supported him.

• On Tom Watson's expression of compassion for Martin but his belief that carts don't belong in an Open.

Martin doesn't agree with Watson, but he understands his viewpoint and holds nothing against him.

• Scott Simpson is against carts as well and stated walking is an integral part of the game. Would Martin explain his position?

Walking would only be an integral part of golf if it would test fatigue. Martin claims what he goes through fulfills the fatigue factor.

• Has the cart issue distracted him from preparing for the Open?

No. It's been what it has been every week. "After six months you're pretty much desensitized to it."

• The USGA ordered a single-rider cart for Martin, but after it malfunctioned twice, Martin was given a regular cart. Since he had said he preferred the regular cart, did the change make him happy?

It did, and while he thinks the single-rider cart is a good idea, it has a few kinks that make it difficult to drive.

• On his reaction to playing in the Open.

He's trying to relax, have fun, and enjoy it, because "You never know if you'll have an experience like this again."

• On his chances of making the 36-hole cut.

"I would be really disappointed if I don't make the cut."

He did indeed make the cut by two strokes. Tied for 26th place after two

rounds, he climbed three places over the last 36 holes and tied for 23rd.

The USGA and Equipment

The following morning, the USGA held its annual press conference, a ritual that had drawn comatose audiences in the past because the USGA had never said anything that awakened the few who slumbered through the ordeal. This time the USGA planned to discuss a hot topic — restricting certain equipment. Not only was everyone there fully alert, the room was jammed and the same television cameras that recorded Martin's interview focused on David B. Fay, the USGA's executive director, Trey Holland, the chairman of the championship committee, which runs the Open, and especially on F. Morgan (Buzz) Taylor, the USGA's president, who had been perceived to have threatened to roll back current technological changes in equipment.

When word got out a month earlier that the USGA would make a statement of substance relating to equipment at the U.S. Open, manufacturers mobilized immediately. Callaway, a publicly traded company, bought full-page advertisements in major newspapers warning the public that the USGA wanted to take away their clubs. *Golf World* amplified the hysteria with a cover picture of Taylor overprinted by the teaser line, "Who is this man and why does he want to take your golf clubs away?"

The USGA's statement seemed mild compared to what had been expected. The significant part of the statement read:

"The United States Golf Association is proposing a test protocol that can objectively measure the 'spring-like' effect in golf club heads. The test will be based on the rebound velocity of a golf ball off a club face. While there may be some exceptions, it is the USGA's expectation and intent that virtually all golf clubs that have been submitted to the USGA will conform to this proposed test."

Fay pointed out that the Rules of Golf state that at impact a club may not have the effect of a spring, or, as some term it, a trampoline effect. The problem now is

A large, attentive audience was on hand for the USGA's press conference regarding equipment.

how to define and measure it. Some years ago the USGA rejected the Reflex, an iron club with a slot behind the face that was calculated to spring the ball farther than a fully solid iron. There was no fuss.

In establishing the standard, an air gun shoots a ball at a stationary plate of titanium about the thickness of most titanium drivers. Sophisticated devices then measure the reaction.

When the standard is finally established, after soliciting comments from manufacturers and other interested parties, followed by an open meeting, the testing procedure is to begin. Once again a ball will be fired from an air gun at an actual club. If the rebound exceeds the standard, the club will not conform to the rules.

Naturally, some manufacturers complained this was not the same as hitting the ball with the club. On the other hand, physicists from the Massachusetts Institute of Technology and Princeton, Lafayette and Lehigh universities believe it is.

Some questions, edited for brevity:
• On whether the standard will be based on clubs that currently conform.

The concern is in what may lie ahead.
• What materials might be coming?

Nobody knows, but the USGA has this opportunity it didn't have before to set a standard that will be applied to all future clubs.

• On the meaning of the acronym BASIC in relation to the USGA's overall equipment testing program.

BASIC stands for biomechanics, aerodynamics (relating to the golf ball), shaft, impact and clubhead. It is a comprehensive program involving experts from the four universities along with the USGA's technical staff.

"It isn't as if we're suddenly deciding to do things," Fay said. "We are an independent regulatory body. It is our responsibility to look at the game and the clubs and balls that are used in it. I think the game would say we have done it well."

• On whether possible lawsuits influence the USGA's conclusions.

No. "We have faced this matter before, and it doesn't influence how we go about our business," Fay said.

• On whether the USGA has consulted manufacturers.

When it is ready, the protocol will be sent to all manufacturers. They may provide written or oral comments, and that will

Ernie Els won earlier at Bay Hill.

Fred Couples had won twice in 1998.

be followed by an open meeting in the fall.

• With respect to the clubs in use now and what may come in the future, how will the USGA determine where to draw the line?

The USGA is talking now about the spring-like effect only. When the manufacturers' comments are weighed and the meeting ended, the USGA will set the standard, that will be the line.

• On whether the USGA has talked about the length of shafts, clubhead size and the number of clubs allowed.

Yes, plenty of talk but no decisions.

• On whether the standard was established to exclude some current clubs and perhaps roll back current technology.

When the USGA set the Overall Distance Standard for the golf ball in 1976, it used the product available at the time. That is why it is basing the new standard on the product in the game today and not basing it on equipment of 20 or 40 years earlier.

The Early Choices

Nothing whets the appetite for glory quite so much as predicting the future and having it all come true — like choosing the winner of the U.S. Open before a ball is struck. The prospects for singling out the

right man in 1998 looked as difficult as ever in the years since Jack Nicklaus slipped back and began playing like everyone else, because so many had played so well.

As an indication of the strength of the Open field, the winners of 17 of the 20 PGA Tour events played so far were ready to tee off. Fred Couples and David Duval led the list.

Both of them had won two tournaments, Couples the Bob Hope Classic and the Memorial Tournament, and Duval at Tucson and Houston. Besides being the only players with two victories, they were running a virtual dead heat atop the PGA Tour's money winners. Couples had won $1,477,017 and Duval $1,462,155, a difference of $14,862, tipping money in these days.

In addition to winning twice, both Couples and Duval could have won the Masters as well. Couples played a poor drive and an even worse 6-iron at Augusta National's 13th hole during the final round and double-bogeyed. Duval missed from 10 feet at the 16th, eight feet at the 17th and 18 feet at the 18th. Mark O'Meara birdied all three and won.

In addition, Duval and Couples had tied for second in the Masters, Duval had finished among the top six in three others, and Couples had tied for second at the GTE Byron Nelson Classic and for third at Houston.

They were among the players given the best chances of winning the Open, along with a few others, including Ernie Els, the defending champion. Els had split his year between the PGA European Tour, which reaches as far as his homeland of South Africa, and the United States. He won twice as well, taking the South African Open and the Bay Hill Invitational in America. One of the crew of players in their 20s who asserted themselves in 1997, Els had won the Open twice by the time he reached 27. Perhaps it was an omen, perhaps not, but Nicklaus had won his second Open at 27.

Justin Leonard had certainly earned consideration, right alongside O'Meara, Davis Love III, Phil Mickelson and the revived Scott Simpson and Tom Watson. Simpson had won the last Open at Olympic in 1987, but 11 years had passed. That was also the last year Watson had a chance on the late holes. Simpson was approaching 43 and Watson had reached 48, but each man had shocked the galleries by winning tournaments in 1998, Simpson at San Diego and Watson at Colonial, four weeks before the Open.

Leonard had won The Players Championship, of course, coming from five strokes behind as he had at Royal Troon when he won the 1997 British Open, tied for second at Tucson and for eighth in both the Masters and Colonial. He ranked third in money winnings, just ahead of Tiger Woods, the biggest draw in golf.

Woods had won as well, beating par by 17 strokes and shooting 271 in Atlanta. He'd placed second twice, tied for third once and tied for eighth in the Masters. Earlier, Woods also won the Johnnie Walker Classic, a PGA European Tour event in Thailand. Like O'Meara, he had a spotty, although brief, record in the Open.

O'Meara's record was grim at best. After tying for third in 1988, he missed the cut in the next six, and tied for 16th and 36th in the next two. Nevertheless, he had

David Duval won at Tucson and Houston.

won the Masters by birdieing the last three holes, tied for second in the small-field Mercedes Championships, the opening tournament of the year, and for third at the Kemper Open in Washington, two weeks before the Open.

Love, perhaps the smoothest swinger in the game, won at Hilton Head, S.C., a favorite hunting ground, as part of a good year, tied for third at San Diego, fifth at the Memorial and seventh at Doral. He had also come down to the last hole at Oakland Hills in 1996 and missed tying Steve Jones by one stroke a year after tying for fourth at Shinnecock Hills.

Above all, though, Tom Lehman and Colin Montgomerie had earned the respect of golfers and fans alike. They'd been close often in the past. Over the previous three years, Lehman had finished third in 1995 and 1997 and tied for second in 1996. Montgomerie had placed third in his debut in 1992, lost a playoff to Els in 1994, and finished second to Els in 1997.

With such experienced players, the galleries could look for a strong field playing a strong course, ideal conditions for a competitive championship.

98th U.S. Open
First Round

While the first round proved nothing, it did indeed demonstrate that common wisdom is often misguiding. There is more to an Open than formula golf.

Ask anyone the key to surviving a U.S. Open and you'll be told you must hit fairways, because if you don't, your ball will lodge in the Open's notorious primary rough — grass so tall and thick it can wrench a club from the hands of even the strongest golfer. Consequently, you'll probably miss the green, and that can mean serious trouble.

Then how could Payne Stewart, playing a course that yielded only grudgingly to the best players in the game, hit only seven of the 14 fairways on driving holes, yet defy logic and hit 14 greens in regulation figures, shoot 66, and shave a severe par by four strokes?

Statistics can be as misleading as common wisdom. Only a few of those misdirected drives settled in the deep rough, and, fortunately, some that did sat up pretty well, leaving him a shot at the green. He also had some luck, playing the last three formidable holes with three birdies.

Stewart's was the lowest opening-round score of any Open at Olympic. Tommy Bolt in 1955, Al Mengert in 1966 and Ben Crenshaw in 1987 all began with 67s. None of them won.

Finding Stewart in the lead could hardly be called a surprise. He had won the 1991 Open, along with the 1989 PGA Championship, and had been among the game's leading players for nearly a decade. Still, his lead couldn't be called safe.

Payne Stewart's (66) accurate approaches enabled him to overcome some loose tee shots.

He led by one stroke over Mark Carnevale, who played the round of his life, birdieing three holes and parring the rest. The son of Ben Carnevale, the former basketball coach at North Carolina and Navy, Mark held second place at 67. Only nine men shot in the 60s. Joe Durant, as obscure as Carnevale, and Tom Lehman, Jose Maria Olazabal and Bob Tway shot 68s, and John Daly, Jeff Maggert and Jesper Parnevik shot 69s.

Close behind, six others shot 70, including Colin Montgomerie, one of the prime choices, Mark O'Meara, the Masters winner, and Matt Kuchar, the U.S. Amateur champion who had played so well at Augusta. Justin Leonard, the British Open champion, and Phil Mickelson shot 71, and Fred Couples shot 72.

At the same time, some others suffered through a grim day. Both Jim Furyk and Tiger Woods shot 74; Ernie Els, still apparently hurting from an episode of back spasms the previous week, birdied only the first hole and shot 75; David Duval shot 75, as well, and at the far reaches of the scoring, Hale Irwin shot 80 and Ben Crenshaw 82.

Olympic had proved itself a very tough course in spite of its lack of length. At 6,797 yards it is the shortest Open course since Merion, near Philadelphia, in 1981, although it is only marginally shorter than Pebble Beach in 1992. A par-72 course, Pebble measured just 6,809 yards.

Still, Olympic presented enough problems to make up for its lack of length. First of all, it is a hilly course that drains energy even from the fittest players as it winds up and down the side of the steep hill. Furthermore, its borders of rough encourage

the players to avoid playing their drivers and use their long irons or fairway woods from the tees. To avoid temptation, Daly left his driver in his locker, even though the equipment firm he represents pays him a substantial bonus for the longest average drive for a season.

Then, its small greens break so severely it is difficult to find suitable hole locations, so putting can be an adventure. Even after play had begun Thursday morning the USGA changed the hole's position at the 18th after realizing a putted ball wouldn't stop near the cup.

While Olympic gave up 305 birdies in the first round, it also claimed 757 bogeys and 150 scores of double bogey or more. Surprising no one, the 17th created the most carnage. While 60 players made their par 4s, 90 scored bogeys or worse. Only five men birdied; Stewart was one of them.

Its three closing holes persistently took away strokes other holes had surrendered. Tom Kite, the 1992 Open champion, stood two under par going to the 16th, made 7, and held on to shoot 70. Steve Pate, the first man off the tee, at 7 o'clock, stood two under going to the 16th as well but finished bogey-bogey-double bogey for 72. Both Stewart Cink and Glen Day were one under going to the 16th and both double-bogeyed the 16th and 17th and shot 73s. Vijay Singh was one under going to the 16th and finished bogey-double bogey-bogey for 73 as well.

Others, of course, played the closing holes better. Aside from Stewart's closing rush, Lehman birdied three of the last four, parring only the 17th, for his 68.

Stewart put up his score early. Paired with Irwin and Curtis Strange, he teed off at 8:20, immediately behind Montgomerie, Furyk and Duval, on a dull, gray and chilly day.

Everyone who lives in the region says coastal San Francisco has a predictable summer climate. The fog that drifts in from the Pacific each morning burns away by

Opposite, the first man off, Steve Pate (72) was also the first to stumble at the finish.

Mark Carnevale (67) played without a bogey.

Joe Durant (68) said his putter saved him.

Bob Tway (68) made pars on the last eight.

Jose Maria Olazabal (68) hit seven fairways.

Tom Lehman (68) birdied three of the last four.

mid-morning and the temperature climbs. But on Thursday a heavy overcast lingered throughout the day, and the temperature settled around 60 degrees, fanned by light winds that occasionally reached 13 mph.

Dressed in what for him was a conservative outfit — navy blue knickers and hose, black shoes, a blue cap and a long-sleeved plaid shirt of blue, red and white — Stewart went out in 34, one under Olympic's par of 35-35–70. Playing scattershot golf, he hit only four fairways and five greens, yet one-putted five holes. He birdied the par-5 first, nearly reaching the green with a 3-wood second shot, but he bogeyed the fourth when his 4-iron drifted right of the green. Missing the fifth green as well, he saved his par by holing from 12 feet, and birdied the little 288-yard seventh with a 2-iron from the tee and a sand wedge to three feet.

Coming back, he hit every green, played the 10th through the 15th in even par, then staged his scoring spurt. At the 609-yard 16th he played a driver, 2-iron and 9-iron to eight feet; at the 17th a driver and 2-iron

First Round

Payne Stewart	66	-4
Mark Carnevale	67	-3
Joe Durant	68	-2
Tom Lehman	68	-2
Jose Maria Olazabal	68	-2
Bob Tway	68	-2
John Daly	69	-1
Jesper Parnevik	69	-1
Jeff Maggert	69	-1

to 45 feet, and at the 18th a 2-iron into the right rough and an 8-iron to 12 feet. He hit not one of those fairways, but he holed every putt and played three devilishly difficult holes in 10 strokes.

The 17th took everything he had to give. Although his drive settled off the fairway, it was eminently playable from the first cut of rough. Stewart told his caddie, "Let's

Jeff Maggert (69) was two over after seven holes.

John Daly (69) played the second nine in 32.

Jesper Parnevik (69) had three birdies.

Davis Love III (78) stumbled to a closing 41.

Colin Montgomerie (70) was frustrated.

chase a 2-iron into the gap. If it gets there, fine. If it doesn't, we'll try to get it up and down."

The shot ran precisely through the gap, pulled up 45 feet past the cup, and Stewart holed the putt.

Speaking later, Stewart said he had played a "really, really, really good round."

He had something to say about the 17th, too.

"I can see birdieing 16 and 18, but if you birdie the 17th you want to soar off that green."

Playing much later in the day, Carnevale birdied the 17th, too. A big, burly 6-foot-2, 238-pounder with a mustache and beard, he played the 17th with a 2-iron second as well and nearly holed it. His ball hit short of the green, brushed through the primary rough, which took some steam off it, then rolled within six inches of the hole.

This was his third birdie. He holed from 45 feet at the eighth, a par 3 of 137 yards, and followed with a 9-iron to 15 feet at the ninth, at 422 yards along a slanting fairway one of the more difficult holes. He might have birdied the 16th, but he missed an uphill five-footer.

Carnevale brought an uninspiring record into the Open. He had played in 15 tournaments in 1998, survived the 36-hole cut in just five, and never placed higher than a tie 41st. The week before the Open he shot 217 in the abbreviated Buick Classic and tied for 63rd. He could not remember the last time he played 18 holes without a bogey.

"It's been awhile; maybe at a Putt-Putt course."

Durant came to San Francisco with only slightly better credentials. He had made the cut in six of his 12 tournaments for the year, and in his best finish tied for 12th at the

Tom Kite (70) made 7 at the 16th hole.

Tom Watson (73) took a double bogey at No. 9.

Houston Open. A Nike Tour graduate, he is the PGA Tour's most accurate driver, hitting 82 percent of the fairways, which should have helped him at Olympic. Even though he missed only three, Durant claimed his putter saved him.

He one-putted seven of the first nine greens, birdied four of the first five holes, and went out in 31, four under par. When he laid a pitching wedge within a foot at the 12th, he led the Open at five under par.

Nerves began to quiver then, and he played loose golf at the 13th, 14th, 16th and 17th, losing three strokes. Other than saving his par after missing the 13th green, he had his lone bright spot at the 15th, another par 3, where he holed from 40 feet.

Durant had never qualified for the Open before; now he stood among the leaders, but with three more grueling rounds to play.

Scott Simpson (72) won here in 1987.

After closing his first round with three consecutive birdies, Payne Stewart opened his second with three more — six consecutive birdies and seven under par for 21 holes over a nerve-taxing course that punished the slightest error. By then he seemed to be staging a rout of the Open, but he knew, as every experienced player in the field knew, that he would not hold on to all those strokes, that eventually he would fall back to the field. Of course he did, and he met his most frustrating moment on the green of the 18th hole.

The USGA had cut the hole in the back left for the opening round, but after looking it over, decided the location was too severe and changed it to a more friendly position. But instead of trying to place the hole on the front of the green all four days, which could cause excessive wear and lead to even more putting trouble, both David Fay, the USGA's executive director, and Tom Meeks, the director of rules and competitions, decided to use the aborted position for the second round. The result ignited colorful criticism and battling putting. Stewart was the most prominent critic, with cause.

By the time he stood on the 18th tee, Stewart had lost all the strokes he had taken early in the round and stood at even par for the day, four under for 35 holes. His pitching wedge settled about 10 feet to the right of the hole, birdie range anywhere else, but not there. He faced a sidehill putt with the green falling away to the left. Caution should have ruled.

Stewart, though, seemed to go too boldly for the hole. His ball eased past on the low side, curled left following the contour of the ground, and kept on rolling. Slowly, very slowly, it ghosted down the slope.

Wearing a look of utter disgust, Stewart walked ahead and stood with his arms crossed in front of him watching the ball creep downhill. When it stopped, it had rolled 20 feet or so below the hole. Stewart got down in two more for bogey and shot 71, still holding the lead.

Stewart's was not the only bizarre incident on the 18th green:

• Playing in the day's first group, Dick Mast laid a pitch within three feet of the hole, but his putt caught the lip, spun out, picked up speed and rolled to the bottom of the green.

• Tom Lehman four-putted.

• Davis Love III's pitch braked six feet above the hole. As soon as he touched the putt he began walking to the collection area on the front to head it off.

• Kevin Wentworth three-putted from five feet and missed the cut.

• In the wackiest act of all, Kirk Triplett blocked his runaway ball with his putter before it glided down the incline, then tapped it in. It cost him a two-stroke penalty, but he would have missed the cut even if he had birdied.

Others, though, escaped without either harm or embarrassment. Omar Uresti rolled his first putt four feet above the hole, and as a USGA official muttered, "He could be right back where he started if he misses this one," he holed out.

Jack Nicklaus holed from 40 feet and shot 74.

Lee Porter had the best solution. A 5-foot-9 North Carolinian playing in his first

Amateur Matt Kuchar (139) chipped in for birdie 2 at the 15th and shot 69.

Payne Stewart (137), shown approaching the 18th green, bogeyed the last two holes.

Bob Tway (138) shot 70 with five birdies.

Open, he holed a 112-yard pitch for an eagle 2 and shot 67, jumping him from a tie for 24th place into a tie for fourth.

While agreeing that the hole location was chancy, Fay said the USGA felt that if the mowing pattern was altered and more water put on the 18th than on the other greens, it would be acceptable. As it turned out, Fay said, "I think it is safe to say that if you were above the hole it was quite difficult. We made a decision and it didn't turn out the way we hoped."

Still steaming as he talked to reporters, Stewart called the hole location borderline ridiculous. Someone asked if the player would have won a free round if he holed the putt. John Daly said maybe they should go to Disney World and play Putt-Putt.

Nicklaus took another view. "To me," he said, "the U.S. Open is a complete examination. Power and accuracy combined

Lee Porter (139) shot 67 to tie for fourth.

Jeff Maggert (138) had his second 69.

Joe Durant (141) said he putted worse.

Lee Janzen (139) posted 66 with a double bogey.

Nick Price (141) tried to be more aggressive.

Second Round

Payne Stewart	66 - 71 – 137	-3
Jeff Maggert	69 - 69 – 138	-2
Bob Tway	68 - 70 – 138	-2
*Matt Kuchar	70 - 69 – 139	-1
Lee Porter	72 - 67 – 139	-1
Lee Janzen	73 - 66 – 139	-1
Mark Carnevale	67 - 73 – 140	E
Joe Durant	68 - 73 – 141	+1
Nick Price	73 - 68 – 141	+1
Brad Faxon	73 - 68 – 141	+1
Stewart Cink	73 - 68 – 141	+1

*Amateur

with touch is what this game is all about — keeping the ball in play and playing the game with discipline. I love disciplined golf."

Lee Janzen agreed, saying, "I come to the U.S. Open expecting nothing to be fair. I expect that if you hit the ball in the rough,

Mark O'Meara (146) fell back with 76.

Brad Faxon (141) said he liked Olympic.

Stewart Cink (141) credited consistent putting.

you can't hit it out. If you hit it into a bunker, you don't have a shot. If you don't hit good shots, you don't make the cut. It's a test of wills to find out who overcomes adversity the best and who has the most patience. It's great. We're professional golfers. We should be tested to the fullest."

Janzen passed the test, shot 66, and with 139 climbed into a tie for fourth place with the amateur Matt Kuchar and Porter, who in his career had played the Asian Tour, the Canadian Tour, the South American Tour, the Japanese Tour and the Nike Tour. Stewart still led with 137, three strokes under par, followed by Jeff Maggert, with his second 69, and Bob Tway, with 68-70, at 138. Both Mark Carnevale, at 140, and Joe Durant, at 141, hung close, and Nick Price, Brad Faxon and Stewart Cink moved up to an eighth-place tie at 141.

Still, Stewart, driving better and yet hitting fewer greens, remained the man to beat, and after his first three holes he gave the distinct impression that he might not be caught. He pitched to 15 feet at the first and holed it, hit two good shots into the second and holed from 15 feet again, played a 5-iron to the third, a 223-yard downhill par 3, and ran the putt home from 25 feet.

Seven under now, his game turned around. He missed the fairways at both the fourth and sixth, took three shots to reach both greens and bogeyed. Two strokes gone; back to one under for the day, four under for 24 holes. A birdie at the seventh won back one of those strokes, and he was out in 33.

Coming back he hit only four fairways and four greens and stumbled in with 38 and 71. His sour finish — three bogeys over the last five holes — left him vulnerable.

Janzen took advantage of it, and considering later developments, made the most significant move. And he did it in spectacular style. He birdied seven holes, bogeyed

Jack Nicklaus (147) made his 35th cut.

Justin Leonard (146) stumbled to 75.

only the sixth, but double-bogeyed the dangerous 17th. Had he parred and followed with another par at the 18th, he'd have tied for the lead. His double bogey didn't exactly wreck his round, but he had just birdied the 15th and 16th and dipped to six under par for the round, three under for 34 holes.

Janzen played a terrific drive on the 17th, long and in the fairway, but his second shot hit a tree and fell into the heavy rough, and his third dropped into a bunker. He came out nicely to six feet, but missed the putt.

"That will teach you," he said. "Don't get greedy. But I imagine I'm not alone in losing shots on that hole."

He was right, indeed. It gave up only three birdies (by Scott Hoch, who didn't make the cut, Steve Stricker and Tiger Woods), 60 pars and 91 scores of bogey or worse.

No matter; Janzen did what he had hoped to do — shoot a sub-par round and climb into contention.

Meantime, while Janzen moved forward, others dropped back. Frustrated after missing the ninth green, Ernie Els took a vicious swipe at the ground, dug up a man-sized divot, and bogeyed, but he followed by holing a full-blooded 8-iron for an eagle 2 at the 10th, shot 70, and had 145 for the 36 holes.

Tom Lehman staggered home in 75, dropping him six strokes behind Stewart. Colin Montgomerie fell back with 74 and 144; John Daly slumped to 75 and 144; Mark O'Meara stumbled to 76 and 145, and Tiger Woods, in danger of missing the cut after a double-bogey 6 at the sixth, came back in 35 with his birdie at the 17th, shot 72, and survived with 146.

Jack Nicklaus survived as well, and, at

Phil Mickelson (144) rested seven strokes back.

58, became the oldest man known to have played all four rounds in a U.S. Open. Nicklaus shot 74 and 147, exactly what he needed. He might have made it by another stroke had Rocky Walcher not parred the 18th by holing a chip from the front of the green. With 70, Walcher became the 60th man to shoot 147 or less. Had he bogeyed, he and 15 others would have survived. His par eliminated some of the best-known names in golf — Tom Watson, Corey Pavin and Hale Irwin, all former Open champions, and all with 148.

Others failed as well. Nick Faldo, who simply didn't putt well, shot 149; Fuzzy Zoeller had 151; Love, having a terrible championship, shot 78-75–153, and Ben Crenshaw, everybody's favorite, stumbled to 82-78–160.

Sixty men had survived, though, but 36 more unrelenting holes lay ahead.

Tiger Woods (146) had "a few loose shots."

Throughout the week, Payne Stewart had insisted that anything around par was a good score at Olympic, which supports the USGA's concept that par is a standard of excellence.

"I keep going back to this," Stewart said. "Any time you make par on a hole and walk off to the next tee, you shouldn't be disappointed."

Analyzing the demands of playing both Olympic and the Open, Stewart said, "You have to shape your shots off the tee. You have to draw the ball, you have to fade the ball. You have to keep the ball in the fairway because you can't play out of the rough. You know that par is going to be a great score."

Par had been hard to beat. While nine men had broken 70 in each of the first two rounds, just three shot in the 60s in the third. Only Tom Lehman and Jeff Maggert had done it twice. Lehman opened with 68, slid to 75 in the second, and bounced back with another 68. Maggert's scores were 69, 69 and 75.

In shooting his second 68, Lehman followed a familiar pattern. His average third-round score in the Opens of 1995 through 1998 is 67, shot at Shinnecock Hills, Oakland Hills, Congressional and Olympic.

At the end of the day he tied Bob Tway for second place at 211, one stroke over par. Only Stewart stood ahead of them, but he led them by four strokes, with Lee Janzen and Nick Price a further stroke behind, at 212.

Stewart was the only man under par for three rounds. With 70 in the third, he had

Tom Lehman (211) birdied the 14th and 18th to make the final pairing for the fourth year.

shot 207, three under. Nine men had been under par for the first 18 holes, six after 36, and now only one after 54. Olympic and the USGA setup had produced a punishing course. It had claimed 328 double bogeys or worse through three rounds. Stewart had made none of them.

By shooting 70, Stewart had lost ground only to Lehman, among the closest challengers. The others fell back. Janzen had a chance to finish closer but once again he double-bogeyed the 17th and shot 73. Tied for second after the second round and two under at the start of the third, Maggert birdied the first but bogeyed the third, double-bogeyed the fifth, bogeyed five more holes, and stumbled to 75.

Of the seven men closest to Stewart at the beginning of the day, only Lehman and Stricker scored under par.

Tied with Janzen and Lee Porter, Matt Kuchar bogeyed the second but then settled down and ran off eight consecutive pars, the kind of golf the Open rewards. Suddenly he lost control, bogeyed five holes on the second nine, came back in 40, shot 76, and dropped into a tie for 10th. Except for a double-bogey 6 at the fifth, Porter played steady golf until the end, where he drove into the rough and double-bogeyed both the 17th and 18th and shot 76. Joe Durant and Brad Faxon shot 76s as well, and Mark Carnevale shot 74.

On a day like this, with so many others throwing away strokes like confetti at a parade, Nick Price could shoot 71 and climb from a tie for eighth into a tie for fourth, five strokes off the lead but within reach. It all depended on whether Stewart could hold on.

Playing under bright skies, in tempera-

Payne Stewart (207) came home with 70 to hold a four-stroke lead entering the final round.

tures close to 70, and swirling winds that edged flying golf balls off line, Stewart raced to the turn in 34, gaining another stroke on par. He struck his biggest blow at the first hole, a downhill par 5 of 533 yards. His drive split the fairway and his 5-iron second settled 18 feet from the hole. He rolled in the putt for an eagle 3. Two under for the day, five under for 37 holes.

The rest of his day, though, was a matter of fighting off every opportunity to collapse. He bunkered his tee shot at the third and bogeyed, left his approach to the fourth short but saved his par with a deft chip to two feet, birdied the eighth with a 7-iron to 18 inches, and drove into the rough at the ninth, couldn't reach the green, and bogeyed again.

He made no birdies at all on the home nine, struggled to save pars on two holes, and bogeyed the 15th, the par 3. His poorly played 7-iron fell into the right greenside bunker and, after recovering, Stewart took two putts from 10 feet.

As his tee shot headed for the bunker, Payne stood fixed as a hunting dog as he watched his shot fly off line. It was easy to see his disgust. As his fellow competitor, Maggert, teed his ball and prepared to play his shot, Stewart moved to the side of the tee and took a number of practice swings hoping to find whatever flaw had crept into his fluid, rhythmic swing.

Then he followed that mistake by miss-

Opposite, Nick Price (212) took a huge swipe of rough to save par at the 14th hole.

Lee Janzen (212) took double bogey at the 17th.

Steve Stricker (213) wanted to reach even par.

ing the 16th fairway, but he still made his par, drove so far he had only a 5-iron second to the 17th but left it short, chipped to four feet and holed it, then played his wedge approach short of the 18th and once again chipped to four feet and holed. In with his 70, Stewart oozed quiet confidence.

Lehman felt confident, too, as well as a bit more settled. After four-putting the 18th the previous day, he had stormed off the course apparently ready to do damage to anyone in his way and taken out some of his frustration on the locker room door.

Calmer the next morning, Lehman admitted, "I was probably as angry as I've ever been coming off a golf course. I had to apologize to a couple of people because I almost bit their heads off."

There was not as much of Lehman as there used to be. Since he played that unlucky shot into the pond surrounding Congressional's 17th green in 1997, he had lost 25 pounds, which must have been a blessing walking hilly Olympic. He had hit

Third Round

Payne Stewart	66 - 71 - 70 – 207 -3
Tom Lehman	68 - 75 - 68 – 211 +1
Bob Tway	68 - 70 - 73 – 211 +1
Nick Price	73 - 68 - 71 – 212 +2
Lee Janzen	73 - 66 - 73 – 212 +2
Steve Stricker	73 - 71 - 69 – 213 +3
Jeff Maggert	69 - 69 - 75 – 213 +3
Stewart Cink	73 - 68 - 73 – 214 +4
Mark Carnevale	67 - 73 - 74 – 214 +4

10 fairways and 11 greens when he shot his second-round 75, but in his third-round 68 he hit only eight fairways and 12 greens.

Starting off an hour before Stewart, Lehman caught his attention by birdieing the

Opposite, Bob Tway (211) could not take advantage of his opportunities on the greens.

These spectators found a great perch at the 16th.

first three holes, holing putts of five feet, four feet and 15 feet. He reached the first with a drive, 6-iron and chip, played an 8-iron into the second, and another 6-iron to the third. A great start, to be sure, but his euphoria didn't last; he drove into the rough at the next three holes, bogeyed them all, and dropped back to where he had been at the beginning.

Out in 35, he dipped under par again when he birdied the 14th by holing a chip after his 8-iron second slid into the secondary rough. Lehman made his last birdie at the 18th, the hole that cost him two strokes the previous day. He drove with a 4-iron and played a pitching wedge to four feet. With the flagstick on the lower level, Lehman holed the putt.

"It was a tough day," he claimed, "but I thought even par would be a good score. It was the same as at Shinnecock, Oakland Hills and Congressional, the kind of day you're trying not to shoot yourself in the foot. When you do that, sometimes good things happen."

Jeff Maggert (213) shot 75, saying "I could have done better … I didn't putt well."

Large, appreciative galleries were on hand every round at The Olympic Club.

Unlike Lehman, Janzen, playing two groups ahead of Stewart, had a rough start. After his opening drive dived into the rough, he carried his second shot over the front-left bunker 10 or 15 yards short of the green and into more rough, hit his third short and into the first cut of rough, chipped to six feet and bogeyed.

Janzen struggled to save par at the second after his drive settled in the high rough and his wedge recovery rolled into a sand-filled divot mark in the fairway, a situation that other players complained about. On with his third, he holed a makeable putt for the 4.

Janzen lost another stroke at the fifth, where he missed the green again — he hadn't hit a fairway yet — chipped poorly, and two-putted from 20 feet, and still another at the ninth, missing another fairway and green and taking three more to get down.

Out in 38, Janzen fought back, birdied the 10th with a sand wedge to less than a foot, the 12th with a 9-iron to a foot and a

Stewart Cink (214) had his second 73.

Matt Kuchar (215) was still enthusiastic.

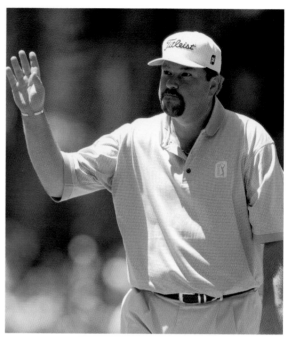

Mark Carnevale (214) maintained a top-10 spot.

Lee Porter (215) had his sights on being "this year's Jack Fleck."

half, and the 15th with a 25-foot putt. By then he had battled back to one over for the day and even par for 51 holes.

He would go no further. Once again the 17th ruined him. After what he called a perfect drive, he drilled a 200-yard 3-iron that raced over the green, and he needed four more shots to hole out — another double bogey. Instead of 33, he shot 35, and with 73 held onto a share of fourth place, but now five strokes behind Stewart rather than two.

"You can't fall asleep out there," Janzen said. "A slight miscue and you can end up with a shot you can't play. I felt like I was into every shot today. I hit good shots and yet I still had four bogeys and a double.

"The guy who plays the best this week and perseveres will get his name on the trophy. They're (the USGA) trying to find a true champion — the guy who overcomes everything, not just hits good shots."

Tom Lehman (211) said the greens were slower.

Payne Stewart (207) made par on the 18th for his 70, "not a bad round of golf today."

Even though Payne Stewart took the biggest lead in 28 years into the final round of the Open, those closest behind him warned that he hadn't won yet, and that he'd probably have to shoot around par to dispel their challenges.

Stewart stood four strokes ahead of Tom Lehman and Bob Tway, the biggest margin since the Englishman Tony Jacklin led Dave Hill by the same amount at Hazeltine in 1970. Jacklin won by seven.

Lee Janzen said, "It won't be easy. He'll still have to play well."

Tway cautioned, "If I were in Payne's position, I wouldn't feel very safe. But if he shoots even par or one over, I don't think we can catch him."

Lehman added, "Payne's having a four-stroke lead makes it easier for the rest of us. We feel a little less pressure and might shoot a good round. When you're sitting on the lead those fairways look like they're an inch wide."

Besides battling the pressure, Stewart had to watch behind him as well. The four men closest to him had all won at least one of the big championships. Janzen had won the 1993 U.S. Open, Lehman the 1996 British Open, Tway the 1986 PGA Championship and Nick Price the 1992 and 1994 PGA Championships and the 1994 British Open. Nevertheless, Stewart seemed confident.

"If I play the way Payne Stewart can play, I'll win the golf tournament," he said. "I'm not going out there to play against Tom Lehman. I'm going to try to play against the golf course. I'm going to take care of Payne Stewart. I can't do anything about

After falling seven strokes behind with 15 holes to play, Lee Janzen (280) rallied to win.

what the others are doing."

Nor could he seem to do anything about what he was doing. Instead of the par round he counted on he shot 74, and Janzen passed him by shooting 68. Janzen finished with 280 and Stewart with 281. Tway took third at 284, Price finished fourth with 285, and Lehman tied Steve Stricker at 286.

His own loose play, along with some luck, cost Stewart the championship. He birdied only one hole and bogeyed five, one of them the 12th, where his drive settled in a sand-filled divot mark. Upset because of his lie, he pushed his approach into a greenside bunker.

That was the bad luck. Janzen had the good luck. His drive at the fifth caught in the branches of a cypress tree and didn't come down. Assuming his ball was lost, Janzen headed back toward the tee to put another ball in play, but he had barely started when a gust of wind fluttered the branches and his ball tumbled down. Had it not, Janzen would have been playing his third shot from the tee. He saved par and turned his game around. After a rocky start, he played the last 15 holes in four under par.

Of the 23 men within 10 strokes of Stewart when the round began, only Janzen played the course under par. Lehman blundered to 75, Tway, Price and Stricker shot 73s, and Jeff Maggert, Stewart Cink, Jim Furyk and Matt Kuchar shot 74s. The finish was especially satisfying for Kuchar, who celebrated his 20th birthday on Sunday. By tying for 14th place, he earned an exemption from qualifying for the 1999 Open at Pinehurst No. 2 in Pinehurst, N.C. His was the best finish by an amateur since Jim Simons nearly won the 1971 championship

Tom Lehman (286) was not a factor on Sunday.

Steve Stricker (286) was paired with Janzen.

at Merion. Simons double-bogeyed the last hole and dropped into a tie for fifth. He tied for 15th at Pebble Beach the following year.

Jack Nicklaus shot 75 and tied for 43rd place with, among others, Tom Kite and Darren Clarke. It was the 42nd consecutive U.S. Open he had graced, and he played better than Ernie Els, the 1997 champion, who had been born two years after Jack had won the second of his four Opens. Els closed with 76 and tied for 49th place in a field of 60.

Five others besides Janzen shot in the 60s. Jeff Sluman shot 68 and advanced from a tie for 39th into a tie for 10th. With 69s, David Duval climbed from a tie for 25th into tie for seventh, and Colin Montgomerie rose from a tie for 44th into a tie for 18th.

Opposite, Bob Tway (284) found the final round a "struggle" as he shot 73 for solo third place.

With his 69, Mark O'Meara climbed from a tie for 54th to a tie for 32nd.

The morning round had barely begun when Paul Azinger showed that Olympic could be tamed. Off in the third pairing, Azinger shot 65 and jumped from a tie for 54th to a tie for 14th. Made up of eight birdies, three bogeys, one on the notorious 17th, and the rest pars, it was the lowest round of the championship, beating the 66s of Stewart in the first round and Janzen in the second. It was also one of only 27 scores under 70 throughout the week.

While others might have seen his blistering round as an indication that the field would tear Olympic apart, Azinger dismissed it, calling it a fluke.

"It's been a long time since I've had a round like that," he said, "but playing early, I had a huge advantage."

Maggert and Cink were the first of the contenders on the course, followed by Jan-

Fourth Round

Lee Janzen	73 - 66 - 73 - 68 – 280	E
Payne Stewart	66 - 71 - 70 - 74 – 281	+1
Bob Tway	68 - 70 - 73 - 73 – 284	+4
Nick Price	73 - 68 - 71 - 73 – 285	+5
Steve Stricker	73 - 71 - 69 - 73 – 286	+6
Tom Lehman	68 - 75 - 68 - 75 – 286	+6
David Duval	75 - 68 - 75 - 69 – 287	+7
Lee Westwood	72 - 74 - 70 - 71 – 287	+7
Jeff Maggert	69 - 69 - 75 - 74 – 287	+7

Lee Westwood (287) rose to a top-10 finish.

zen and Stricker, then Tway and Price, then Stewart and Lehman.

Under overcast skies once again, the weather had cooled since Saturday, and a slight wind blew in from the Pacific. Playing in pleasant conditions, Maggert birdied the first, but he bogeyed three holes of the first nine and never threatened. Nor did Cink, who birdied the second but then ran off three consecutive bogeys.

Price, who had hit more fairways and greens than anyone in the field through the first three rounds, simply couldn't hole a putt, didn't make a single birdie, and played no part in the result. Nor did Tway, who couldn't recover from two opening bogeys.

Everyone expected more of Lehman. Playing in the last pairing for the fourth consecutive year, he had gone down to the last hole in 1996 but lost to Steve Jones, and to the 17th in 1997, losing to Els. While his followers expected great things, Lehman disappointed them. His troubles began at the first hole.

No one of his caliber normally bogeys Olympic's first, a par 5 within reach of an iron-club second. Lehman hit a wild drive and fumbled his way to a bogey 6 on a hole that surrendered 163 birdies and seven eagles, 103 more sub-par scores than the eighth, the next-easiest par.

After saving a par at the second, where

Opposite, Nick Price (285) three-putted twice in the final six holes to ruin his chances.

Jeff Sluman (288) shot 68 with a good start.

Stuart Appleby (288) shot 71 and moved up.

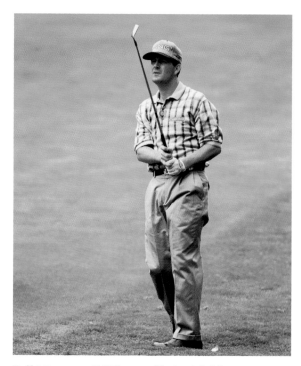

Jeff Maggert (287) stumbled with his 74.

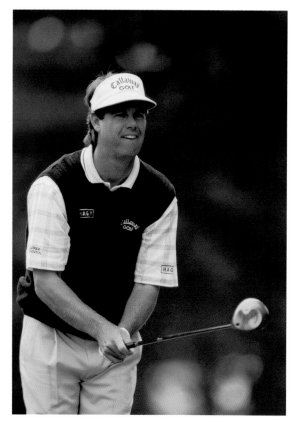

Paul Azinger (289) called his 65 a fluke.

his drive drifted into the heavy rough, Lehman had a chance at a birdie with a solid tee shot at the third. Instead, he hit a weak first putt and a timid second that wobbled into the hole. He never made a move and didn't birdie one hole.

While Lehman plodded, Stewart showed nothing either. He had played the first hole with two birdies and an eagle through the first three rounds, but with the Open waiting to be won, he parred.

Even so, he gained ground on nearly everyone, for not only had Lehman blundered, Janzen had missed both the second and third greens, bogeyed them both, and fallen seven strokes behind Stewart.

From that point on, though, Janzen played relentless, often attacking, golf. He rifled a 5-iron to 20 feet at the fourth and holed a teasing putt that broke about two feet. One birdie, six strokes behind now.

Then he had his incident with the tree. Reprieved when his ball fell, Janzen chopped it back to the fairway, overshot the green with a 6-iron third, then holed his chip for the par.

The incident seemed spooky, bringing

Payne Stewart (281) blasted his fourth shot from a bunker on No. 16 and scored a bogey 6.

back memories of Baltusrol in 1993, where Janzen won his first Open. Playing the 10th hole, he pushed his drive in the rough behind a pair of tall, billowing oaks. Trying to play over them, he mis-hit his iron, the ball took off directly at the upper branches and sailed directly through, as far as anyone knows, without disturbing a leaf. Later, at the 16th, he holed a chip and birdied. Now he had repeated 1993.

About 15 minutes later, Stewart had his own trouble with a tree. When he yanked his drive well left at the fourth, his ball banged against a towering pine and caromed toward the fairway rather than into the woods. It cost him a bogey. Five ahead now, two strokes lost to Janzen. No one else mattered. As they had at Baltusrol, they would settle the championship themselves.

Playing steadily now, Janzen birdied the seventh with a sand wedge to six feet and picked up another stroke. Four strokes behind now, Janzen closed to within three when Stewart bogeyed the seventh after pitching to a dangerous position on the two-tiered green. With his ball on the upper level and the hole on the lower level,

Janzen reached even par with his birdie at No. 13.

49

A 20-foot birdie putt at No. 18 was Stewart's last chance to win this year's championship.

Stewart faced a terrifying putt that must ghost down the slope and break sharply left. In honesty, the putt was impossible.

When Stewart took his stance, his back nearly turned toward the hole, he tapped the ball softly, only enough to start it rolling. It glided down the hill, took the break, and coasted six feet or more past the hole. He three-putted. In seven holes he had lost two strokes to par. More trouble was coming.

With another stroke of luck, Janzen birdied the 11th, where his approach kicked off a hillock and rolled eight feet from the hole, and the 13th where a 5-iron rolled to five feet. Janzen had climbed back to even par for the distance, within one stroke of Stewart. Within the next half hour, Stewart bogeyed both the 12th and 13th, falling one stroke behind Janzen, still playing two holes ahead. Every one of Stewart's strokes had gone, even though he birdied the 14th, pulling himself back into a tie.

Janzen certainly couldn't relax; he still had three hard holes to play. He played them the way they had to be played. He hit every fairway and every green, and for once

he parred the 17th. In his three previous rounds he had bogeyed once and double-bogeyed twice, but with the Open hanging on every shot, Janzen attacked. He powered a stunning drive that streaked down the left side of the fairway, then ripped a 3-iron through the gap to the back of the green. Two putts and he had his par.

Another loosely played 7-iron into the green of the 609-yard 16th soured Stewart's hopes. After missing the fairway and chopping a 5-iron out of the rough, once again he bunkered the approach. He bogeyed and fell one behind again.

Stewart had one more chance, and he nearly pulled it off. His 20-foot putt at the 18th ran toward the hole, and for a heart-stopping moment looked as if it would fall. Just as it had almost reached the hole, it turned away and missed. Janzen had won.

Janzen finished with 280, even par for the 72 holes.

Par had indeed been established as the standard of excellence.

Janzen acknowledged the applause for his effort.

98th U.S. Open

The Champion

In one of the more illogical situations that occurred at the top levels of professional golf during the year, Lee Janzen was paired with Payne Stewart in the opening round of the Western Open one week after Lee had beaten Payne and won the U.S. Open, the biggest prize of all. While Janzen called it "somewhat awkward," it didn't seem to affect his game. He shot another 68 and Stewart shot 72. Still in euphoric shock from winning the Open, Janzen shot 277 and tied Dudley Hart for third place behind Joe Durant, the winner, and Vijay Singh. After some hard times, Janzen seemed well into rehab.

A year ago, when Ernie Els won the Open and the Buick Classic the following week, he rose to the top of the World Ranking. Janzen made no such climb. He was ranked 42nd before the Open began, and 21st when the Western ended. Not especially significant, but he'd had his best two weeks in years.

There seemed to have been a certain similarity between Janzen and Els after they won their first U.S. Opens (Els had won in 1994, Janzen in 1993). Els was capable of playing sensational golf one week and indifferently the next. Before he won his second Open at Congressional last year, he had played especially well in Europe and South Africa, his home country, but not as well in the United States.

Those who watch the game closely believed they saw a similar pattern in Janzen, because when he first broke into golf's highest levels, he looked to be one of the game's blossoming stars. He caught everyone's attention early in 1993 by winning at Phoenix, placing sixth at Pebble Beach and Greensboro, seventh at the Kemper Open

and third at Westchester. Then he played four rounds in the 60s at Baltusrol, shot 272, matched the 72-hole record, and beat Stewart by two strokes. Over the next two years he won four more tournaments.

Coming into the Open at Olympic, though, Janzen hadn't won since taking the Sprint International in August 1995. In the next three seasons, Janzen finished as high as second in only three tournaments, third in one other and tied for fourth in Houston early in May 1998. Not that he was washed up; he still made a very nice living playing the game. He placed third on the money-winning list in 1995, 31st in 1996, 24th in 1997, and his performances in the Open and the Western jumped him to sixth place midway through 1998.

Again like Els, he'd had a few dismaying failures. Els had the 1995 PGA Championship practically won after three rounds, but he played a wobbly 72 in the fourth and dropped to third. Earlier in 1998, Janzen held a three-stroke lead after three rounds of The Players Championship but blundered to 79 in the fourth and dropped into a tie for 13th place. Late losses like that made him wonder, "Am I going to win again?"

It was a scary thought, but Janzen fought it off by telling himself, "You have to take the attitude that you don't care how long it takes to win, but that you just know you're going to win again. You just work hard and get your game as good as you can. Then, when the opportunity comes up, you can take advantage of it."

Janzen confessed that he may have

Lee Janzen became the 18th player to win the U.S. Open more than once.

The gallery around the 18th hole at Olympic enjoyed four days of excellent weather and golf.

caused his own troubles because winning his first Open might have raised his expectations too high. He was 28 years old in 1993, and relatively inexperienced.

"I didn't know what to expect of myself and what the demands would be," he explained. "Suddenly I became noticed, and my game fell off. Maybe it was because I had risen to a level where I'd never been. It was hard to maintain that level."

Asked if he believed his second Open will become more important that his first, he answered, "I think so. I think it elevates what I've done to a whole new level."

Janzen was 33 when he won at Olympic. He was born in Minnesota and spent his boyhood in Maryland, where he played

Little League ball and became a compulsive fan of the Baltimore Orioles. He took up golf at the age of 14 when his family moved to Florida.

He is a slender six feet tall, wears a baseball-type cap that covers his wavy, reddish hair and seems to change logos every year. Like his cap, he switches his brand of clubs almost annually.

He's also emotional, a quality he used to drive himself in the last round at Olympic. After he birdied the 11th and climbed within two strokes of Stewart, he prodded himself with the thought, "This is the U.S. Open, and I have a chance to win."

"I had to keep reminding myself that it only takes one bad shot to lose. When I lose focus I could ruin any chance of winning. That's what kept me going. I just said that I can't relax and think about all the great things until this is over. If you don't give every shot your full attention, you're not going to win this thing."

Later, as he cradled the silver U.S. Open Championship trophy, he brushed a tear from his eye.

Unlike Els, Janzen doesn't look especially athletic. While Els' swing flows like liquid, Janzen's appears less natural. He walks in a stiff-appearing gait, and when he bends from the waist to putt, his knees look rigid.

That doesn't mean he can't hit the ball, and it certainly doesn't mean he can't putt. In an Open where three putts were common and four putts no longer news, Janzen three-putted only the sixth hole of the second round and had a total of 118 putts, ranking 21st in the field. He birdied 15 holes, bogeyed 11, and double-bogeyed the 17th twice.

Janzen won because he played such exacting golf. On a course whose slanted fairways kicked well-struck drives into the rough, Janzen held his ball on 40 fairways, third-best in the field; and while he's not thought of as one of the game's long hitters, he averaged 281 yards on selected holes, 11th best.

Most important, perhaps, he hit and held 50 of those small, tightly guarded, undulating greens, one more than Nick Price, who ranked second.

Stewart recognized how well Janzen had played.

Waving a sheet of paper, Payne said, "Let me just show you something right here. Now I hit six fairways today and Lee Janzen hit 11. I hit nine greens and Lee Janzen hit 14. Bingo! That's why I didn't win."

In the midst of the frenzy swirling around him, and the glamour of it all, Janzen was asked if he guards against considering himself a great player now.

"I guess it's all in your interpretation of what it takes to be a great player," he answered. "I still don't put myself in the same category as other guys. Some of them play unbelievably well."

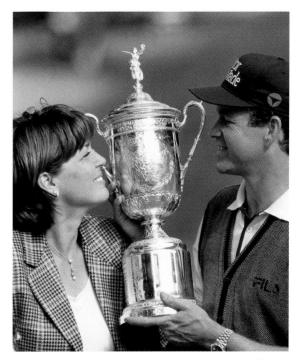

Janzen and his wife Beverly.

Nevertheless, Janzen moved into select company at Olympic. This was the 98th U.S. Open. He is one of just 18 men who have won it more than once. He is also one of two men who have won the Open twice in this decade (the other is Els, of course, in 1994 and 1997).

Janzen believes his second Open, the eighth win of his career, could have broad consequences. "I think it completely erases my bad tournaments and my not winning for three years," he said. "Now I've won eight in just under nine years. I can't be too upset."

Suppose this, his eighth victory, had been a PGA Tour event; would it have had the same significance?

"I don't know that it would have had anywhere near the significance," he answered.

Asked why not, he said, "Because the trophy says United States Open on it. Being an American, it has more special meaning than any other tournament. I just think this is the best to win. I've won it twice. Life doesn't get any better, because that's the best I can do."

98th U.S. Open

June 18-21, 1998, The Olympic Club, San Francisco, California

Contestant	Rounds				Total	Prize
Lee Janzen	73	66	73	68	280	$535,000.00
Payne Stewart	66	71	70	74	281	315,000.00
Bob Tway	68	70	73	73	284	201,730.00
Nick Price	73	68	71	73	285	140,597.00
Steve Stricker	73	71	69	73	286	107,392.00
Tom Lehman	68	75	68	75	286	107,392.00
David Duval	75	68	75	69	287	83,794.00
Lee Westwood	72	74	70	71	287	83,794.00
Jeff Maggert	69	69	75	74	287	83,794.00
Jeff Sluman	72	74	74	68	288	64,490.00
Phil Mickelson	71	73	74	70	288	64,490.00
Stuart Appleby	73	74	70	71	288	64,490.00
Stewart Cink	73	68	73	74	288	64,490.00
Paul Azinger	75	72	77	65	289	52,214.00
Jesper Parnevik	69	74	76	70	289	52,214.00
*Matt Kuchar	70	69	76	74	289	Medal
Jim Furyk	74	73	68	74	289	52,214.00
Colin Montgomerie	70	74	77	69	290	41,833.00
Loren Roberts	71	76	71	72	290	41,833.00
Tiger Woods	74	72	71	73	290	41,833.00
Frank Lickliter	73	71	72	74	290	41,833.00
Jose Maria Olazabal	68	77	71	74	290	41,833.00
Casey Martin	74	71	74	72	291	34,043.00
Glen Day	73	72	71	75	291	34,043.00
D.A. Weibring	72	72	75	73	292	25,640.00
Per-Ulrik Johansson	71	75	73	73	292	25,640.00
Eduardo Romero	72	70	76	74	292	25,640.00
Vijay Singh	73	72	73	74	292	25,640.00
Chris Perry	74	71	72	75	292	25,640.00
Thomas Bjorn	72	75	70	75	292	25,640.00
Mark Carnevale	67	73	74	78	292	25,640.00
Mark O'Meara	70	76	78	69	293	18,372.00
Padraig Harrington	73	72	76	72	293	18,372.00
Steve Pate	72	75	73	73	293	18,372.00
Bruce Zabriski	74	71	74	74	293	18,372.00
Joe Durant	68	73	76	76	293	18,372.00
John Huston	73	72	72	76	293	18,372.00
Chris DiMarco	71	71	74	77	293	18,372.00
Lee Porter	72	67	76	78	293	18,372.00
Justin Leonard	71	75	77	71	294	15,155.00
Scott McCarron	72	73	77	72	294	15,155.00
Frank Nobilo	76	67	76	75	294	15,155.00
Darren Clarke	74	72	77	72	295	12,537.00
Tom Kite	70	75	76	74	295	12,537.00
Joe Acosta	73	72	76	74	295	12,537.00

Contestant	Rounds				Total	Prize
Joey Sindelar	71	75	75	74	295	12,537.00
Olin Browne	73	70	77	75	295	12,537.00
Jack Nicklaus	73	74	73	75	295	12,537.00
Ernie Els	75	70	75	76	296	9,711.00
Michael Reid	76	70	73	77	296	9,711.00
Scott Verplank	74	72	73	77	296	9,711.00
Brad Faxon	73	68	76	79	296	9,711.00
Jim Johnson	74	73	79	71	297	8,531.00
Fred Couples	72	75	79	71	297	8,531.00
Tim Herron	75	72	77	73	297	8,531.00
John Daly	69	75	75	78	297	8,531.00
Mark Brooks	75	71	76	76	298	8,030.00
Scott Simpson	72	71	78	79	300	7,844.00
Rocky Walcher	77	70	77	79	303	7,696.00
Tom Sipula	75	71	78	81	305	7,549.00

Derek Gilchrist	74	74	148	Christian Chernock	73	77	150	Shane Bertsch	77	77	154
Corey Pavin	76	72	148	Mark Wilson	74	76	150	Perry Parker	75	79	154
Billy Andrade	74	74	148	Willie Wood	74	76	150	Martin Lonardi	76	78	154
* Paul Simson	76	72	148	Clarence Rose	75	75	150	Costantino Rocca	71	83	154
Jay Haas	76	72	148	Sam Randolph	80	70	150	Perry Moss	76	78	154
Gene Fieger	76	72	148	Jimmy Green	76	74	150	Curtis Strange	77	78	155
Brent Geiberger	71	77	148	Mark Calcavecchia	74	76	150	* Ryan Palmer	82	73	155
Grant Waite	77	71	148	Phil Tataurangi	77	73	150	Chip Beck	78	77	155
Patrick Lee	72	76	148	Grant Clough	78	73	151	Ted Oh	74	81	155
Andrew Magee	70	78	148	Don Pooley	74	77	151	Wes Weston	79	76	155
Hale Irwin	80	68	148	Ian Woosnam	72	79	151	Rick Gehr	73	82	155
Tom Watson	73	75	148	Fuzzy Zoeller	75	76	151	Rick Todd	80	76	156
John Cook	75	73	148	Dick Mast	76	76	152	Guy Boros	77	79	156
Retief Goosen	74	74	148	Graham Marsh	75	77	152	Chris Tidland	76	80	156
Brad Fabel	75	73	148	* Vaughn Taylor	76	76	152	Gary March	76	81	157
Omar Uresti	78	71	149	Tim Straub	74	78	152	Mike Burke, Jr.	81	76	157
Doug Martin	74	75	149	Tom Sutter	79	73	152	* Joel Kribel	83	75	158
Steve Jones	72	77	149	Kirk Triplett	73	79	152	Jeff Thorsen	77	81	158
Nick Faldo	77	72	149	Robert Deruntz	75	77	152	Brett Wetterich	78	80	158
Briny Baird	75	74	149	Brandel Chamblee	76	77	153	Ken Peyreferry	80	79	159
Edward Fryatt	73	76	149	Bernhard Langer	75	78	153	Garrett Larson	80	79	159
* David Eger	78	71	149	Kevin Sutherland	77	76	153	Ben Crenshaw	82	78	160
Scott Hoch	74	75	149	Mike Brisky	74	79	153	Howard Twitty	79	81	160
Paul Stankowski	76	73	149	Garrett Willis	83	70	153	Alan Morin	80	82	162
Masashi Ozaki	78	71	149	Jason Gore	77	76	153	Jimmy Johnston	84	78	162
Gary Hallberg	77	72	149	Davis Love III	78	75	153	Rene Rangel	82	81	163
Kevin Wentworth	76	73	149	Pete Jordan	81	72	153	Jeff McMillian	82	81	163
Chris Kaufman	77	72	149	Mike Small	76	77	153	Tom Anderson	84	80	164
David Kirkpatrick	78	72	150	Jason Allen	76	78	154	Adrian Stills	85	81	166
Trevor Dodds	74	76	150	Ignacio Garrido	76	78	154	Richard Ames	86	81	167
Steve Elkington	77	73	150	Jim Estes	77	77	154				
David Ogrin	70	80	150	Robert Karlsson	78	76	154				

Professionals not returning 72-hole scores received $1,000 each.

*Denotes amateur.

98th
U.S. Open
Statistics

Hole	1	2	3	4	5	6	7	8	9	10	11	12	13	14	15	16	17	18	Total
Par	5	4	3	4	4	4	4	3	4	4	4	4	3	4	3	5	4	4	70

Lee Janzen

	1	2	3	4	5	6	7	8	9	10	11	12	13	14	15	16	17	18	Total	
Round 1	5	4	[4]	4	4	4	(3)	3	[5]	4	4	[5]	3	4	3	5	[5]	4	73	
Round 2	(4)	4	(2)	4	4	[5]	4	(2)	(3)	4	(3)	4	3	4	(2)	(4)	[6]	4	66	
Round 3	[6]	4	3	4	[5]	4	4	3	[5]	(3)	4	(3)	3	[5]	(2)	5	[6]	4	73	
Round 4	5	[5]	[4]	(3)	4	4	(3)	3	4	4	(3)	4	(2)	4	3	5	4	4	68	280

Payne Stewart

	1	2	3	4	5	6	7	8	9	10	11	12	13	14	15	16	17	18	Total	
Round 1	(4)	4	3	[5]	4	4	(3)	3	4	4	4	4	3	4	3	(4)	(3)	(3)	66	
Round 2	(4)	(3)	(2)	[5]	4	[5]	(3)	3	4	4	4	4	3	[5]	3	5	[5]	[5]	71	
Round 3	(3)	4	[4]	4	4	4	4	(2)	[5]	4	4	4	3	4	[4]	5	4	4	70	
Round 4	5	4	3	[5]	4	4	[5]	3	4	4	4	[5]	[4]	(3)	3	[6]	4	4	74	281

Bob Tway

	1	2	3	4	5	6	7	8	9	10	11	12	13	14	15	16	17	18	Total	
Round 1	(4)	[5]	(2)	4	[5]	(3)	4	3	4	(3)	4	4	3	4	3	5	4	4	68	
Round 2	(4)	4	3	4	[5]	(3)	(3)	[4]	4	[5]	4	4	[4]	(3)	3	5	[5]	(3)	70	
Round 3	5	(3)	3	4	4	4	[5]	3	[6]	4	4	4	[4]	4	3	5	[5]	(3)	73	
Round 4	[6]	[5]	3	4	4	4	(3)	3	[5]	4	4	[5]	3	4	3	5	4	4	73	284

O Circled numbers represent birdies or eagles.   □ Squared numbers represent bogeys or double bogeys.

Hole	Yards	Par	Eagles	Birdies	Pars	Bogeys	Higher	Average
1	533	5	7	163	201	52	6	4.741
2	394	4	0	35	246	127	21	4.322
3	223	3	0	37	251	129	12	3.273
4	438	4	0	26	206	164	33	4.483
5	457	4	0	33	207	154	35	4.452
6	437	4	0	37	260	120	12	4.252
7	288	4	2	90	247	76	14	4.033
8	137	3	0	67	303	54	5	2.993
9	433	4	0	44	232	135	18	4.298
OUT	3,340	35	9	532	2,153	1,011	156	36.847
10	422	4	1	47	276	90	15	4.170
11	430	4	0	37	250	128	14	4.277
12	416	4	0	35	257	114	23	4.294
13	186	3	1	31	266	118	13	3.261
14	422	4	0	34	249	118	28	4.336
15	157	3	0	58	269	86	16	3.142
16	609	5	0	47	256	99	27	5.254
17	468	4	0	9	166	198	56	4.716
18	347	4	1	67	235	102	24	4.196
IN	3,457	35	3	365	2,224	1,053	216	37.646
TOTAL	6,797	70	12	897	4,377	2,064	372	74.493

Date	Winner	Score	Runner-Up	Venue
1895	Horace Rawlins	173 - 36 holes	Willie Dunn	Newport GC, Newport, RI
1896	James Foulis	152 - 36 holes	Horace Rawlins	Shinnecock Hills GC, Southampton, NY
1897	Joe Lloyd	162 - 36 holes	Willie Anderson	Chicago GC, Wheaton, IL
1898	Fred Herd	328 - 72 holes	Alex Smith	Myopia Hunt Club, S. Hamilton, MA
1899	Willie Smith	315	George Low Val Fitzjohn W.H. Way	Baltimore CC, Baltimore, MD
1900	Harry Vardon	313	J.H. Taylor	Chicago GC, Wheaton, IL
1901	*Willie Anderson (85)	331	Alex Smith (86)	Myopia Hunt Club, S. Hamilton, MA
1902	Laurie Auchterlonie	307	Stewart Gardner	Garden City GC, Garden City, NY
1903	*Willie Anderson (82)	307	David Brown (84)	Baltusrol GC, Springfield, NJ
1904	Willie Anderson	303	Gil Nicholls	Glen View Club, Golf, IL
1905	Willie Anderson	314	Alex Smith	Myopia Hunt Club, S. Hamilton, MA
1906	Alex Smith	295	Willie Smith	Onwentsia Club, Lake Forest, IL
1907	Alex Ross	302	Gil Nicholls	Philadelphia Cricket Club, Chestnut Hill, PA
1908	*Fred McLeod (77)	322	Willie Smith (83)	Myopia Hunt Club, S. Hamilton, MA
1909	George Sargent	290	Tom McNamara	Englewood GC, Englewood, NJ
1910	*Alex Smith (71)	298	John J. McDermott (75) Macdonald Smith (77)	Philadelphia Cricket Club, Chestnut Hill, PA
1911	*John J. McDermott (80)	307	Michael J. Brady (82) George O. Simpson (85)	Chicago GC, Wheaton, IL
1912	John J. McDermott	294	Tom McNamara	CC of Buffalo, Buffalo, NY
1913	*Francis Ouimet (72)	304	Harry Vardon (77) Edward Ray (78)	The Country Club, Brookline, MA
1914	Walter Hagen	290	Charles Evans, Jr.	Midlothian CC, Blue Island, IL
1915	Jerome D. Travers	297	Tom McNamara	Baltusrol GC, Springfield, NJ
1916	Charles Evans, Jr.	286	Jock Hutchinson	Minikahda Club, Minneapolis, MN
1917-18	No Championships Played — World War I			
1919	*Walter Hagen (77)	301	Michael J. Brady (78)	Brae Burn CC, West Newton, MA
1920	Edward Ray	295	Harry Vardon Jack Burke, Sr. Leo Diegel Jock Hutchison	Inverness Club, Toledo, OH
1921	James M. Barnes	289	Walter Hagen Fred McLeod	Columbia CC, Chevy Chase, MD
1922	Gene Sarazen	288	John L. Black Robert T. Jones, Jr.	Skokie CC, Glencoe, IL
1923	*Robert T. Jones, Jr. (76)	296	Bobby Cruickshank (78)	Inwood CC, Inwood, NY
1924	Cyril Walker	297	Robert T. Jones, Jr.	Oakland Hills CC, Birmingham, MI
1925	*William MacFarlane (147)	291	Robert T. Jones, Jr. (148)	Worcester CC, Worcester, MA
1926	Robert T. Jones, Jr.	293	Joe Turnesa	Scioto CC, Columbus, OH
1927	*Tommy Armour (76)	301	Harry Cooper (79)	Oakmont CC, Oakmont, PA
1928	*Johnny Farrell (143)	294	Robert T. Jones, Jr. (144)	Olympia Fields CC, Matteson, IL
1929	*Robert T. Jones, Jr. (141)	294	Al Espinosa (164)	Winged Foot GC, Mamaroneck, NY
1930	Robert T. Jones, Jr.	287	Macdonald Smith	Interlachen CC, Hopkins, MN

Date	Winner	Score	Runner-Up	Venue
1931	*Billy Burke (149-148)	292	George Von Elm (149-149)	Inverness Club, Toledo, OH
1932	Gene Sarazen	286	Phil Perkins	Fresh Meadows CC, Flushing, NY
			Bobby Cruickshank	
1933	Johnny Goodman	287	Ralph Guldahl	North Shore CC, Glenview, IL
1934	Olin Dutra	293	Gene Sarazen	Merion Cricket Club, Ardmore, PA
1935	Sam Parks, Jr.	299	Jimmy Thomson	Oakmont CC, Oakmont, PA
1936	Tony Manero	282	Harry Cooper	Baltusrol GC, Springfield, NJ
1937	Ralph Guldahl	281	Sam Snead	Oakland Hills CC, Birmingham, MI
1938	Ralph Guldahl	284	Dick Metz	Cherry Hills CC, Englewood, CO
1939	*Byron Nelson (68-70)	284	Craig Wood (68-73)	Philadelphia CC, West
			Denny Shute (76)	Conshohocken, PA
1940	*Lawson Little (70)	287	Gene Sarazen (73)	Canterbury GC, Cleveland, OH
1941	Craig Wood	284	Denny Shute	Colonial Club, Fort Worth, TX
1942-45	No Championships Played — World War II			
1946	*Lloyd Mangrum (72-72)	284	Vic Ghezzi (72-73)	Canterbury GC, Cleveland, OH
			Byron Nelson (72-73)	
1947	*Lew Worsham (69)	282	Sam Snead (70)	St. Louis CC, Clayton, MO
1948	Ben Hogan	276	Jimmy Demaret	Riviera CC, Los Angeles, CA
1949	Cary Middlecoff	286	Sam Snead	Medinah CC, Medinah, IL
			Clayton Heafner	
1950	*Ben Hogan (69)	287	Lloyd Mangrum (73)	Merion GC, Ardmore, PA
			George Fazio (75)	
1951	Ben Hogan	287	Clayton Heafner	Oakland Hills CC, Birmingham, MI
1952	Julius Boros	281	Ed (Porky) Oliver	Northwood CC, Dallas, TX
1953	Ben Hogan	283	Sam Snead	Oakmont CC, Oakmont, PA
1954	Ed Furgol	284	Gene Littler	Baltusrol GC, Springfield, NJ
1955	*Jack Fleck (69)	287	Ben Hogan (72)	The Olympic Club, San Francisco, CA
1956	Cary Middlecoff	281	Ben Hogan	Oak Hill CC, Rochester, NY
			Julius Boros	
1957	*Dick Mayer (72)	282	Cary Middlecoff (79)	Inverness Club, Toledo, OH
1958	Tommy Bolt	283	Gary Player	Southern Hills CC, Tulsa, OK
1959	Billy Casper	282	Bob Rosburg	Winged Foot GC, Mamaroneck, NY
1960	Arnold Palmer	280	Jack Nicklaus	Cherry Hills CC, Englewood, CO
1961	Gene Littler	281	Bob Goalby	Oakland Hills CC, Birmingham, MI
			Doug Sanders	
1962	*Jack Nicklaus (71)	283	Arnold Palmer (74)	Oakmont CC, Oakmont, PA
1963	*Julius Boros (70)	293	Jacky Cupit (73)	The Country Club, Brookline, MA
			Arnold Palmer (76)	
1964	Ken Venturi	278	Tommy Jacobs	Congressional CC, Bethesda, MD
1965	*Gary Player (71)	282	Kel Nagle (74)	Bellerive CC, St. Louis, MO
1966	*Billy Casper (69)	278	Arnold Palmer (73)	The Olympic Club, San Francisco, CA
1967	Jack Nicklaus	275	Arnold Palmer	Baltusrol GC, Springfield, NJ
1968	Lee Trevino	275	Jack Nicklaus	Oak Hill CC, Rochester, NY
1969	Orville Moody	281	Deane Beman	Champions GC, Houston, TX
			Al Geiberger	
			Bob Rosburg	
1970	Tony Jacklin	281	Dave Hill	Hazeltine National GC, Chaska, MN
1971	*Lee Trevino (68)	280	Jack Nicklaus (71)	Merion GC, Ardmore, PA
1972	Jack Nicklaus	290	Bruce Crampton	Pebble Beach GL, Pebble Beach, CA
1973	Johnny Miller	279	John Schlee	Oakmont CC, Oakmont, PA
1974	Hale Irwin	287	Forrest Fezler	Winged Foot GC, Mamaroneck, NY
1975	*Lou Graham (71)	287	John Mahaffey (73)	Medinah CC, Medinah, IL
1976	Jerry Pate	277	Tom Weiskopf	Atlanta Athletic Club, Duluth, GA
			Al Geiberger	

Date	Winner	Score	Runner-Up	Venue
1977	Hubert Green	278	Lou Graham	Southern Hills CC, Tulsa, OK
1978	Andy North	285	Dave Stockton	Cherry Hills CC, Englewood, CO
			J.C. Snead	
1979	Hale Irwin	284	Gary Player	Inverness Club, Toledo, OH
			Jerry Pate	
1980	Jack Nicklaus	272	Isao Aoki	Baltusrol GC, Springfield, NJ
1981	David Graham	273	George Burns	Merion GC, Ardmore, PA
			Bill Rogers	
1982	Tom Watson	282	Jack Nicklaus	Pebble Beach GL, Pebble Beach, CA
1983	Larry Nelson	280	Tom Watson	Oakmont CC, Oakmont, PA
1984	*Fuzzy Zoeller (67)	276	Greg Norman (75)	Winged Foot GC, Mamaroneck, NY
1985	Andy North	279	Dave Barr	Oakland Hills CC, Birmingham, MI
			Chen Tze Chung	
			Denis Watson	
1986	Raymond Floyd	279	Lanny Wadkins	Shinnecock Hills GC,
			Chip Beck	Southampton, NY
1987	Scott Simpson	277	Tom Watson	The Olympic Club, San Francisco, CA
1988	*Curtis Strange (71)	278	Nick Faldo (75)	The Country Club, Brookline, MA
1989	Curtis Strange	278	Chip Beck	Oak Hill CC, Rochester, NY
			Mark McCumber	
			Ian Woosnam	
1990	*Hale Irwin (74+3)	280	Mike Donald (74+4)	Medinah CC, Medinah, IL
1991	*Payne Stewart (75)	282	Scott Simpson (77)	Hazeltine National GC, Chaska, MN
1992	Tom Kite	285	Jeff Sluman	Pebble Beach GL, Pebble Beach, CA
1993	Lee Janzen	272	Payne Stewart	Baltusrol GC, Springfield, NJ
1994	*Ernie Els (74+4+4)	279	Loren Roberts (74+4+5)	Oakmont CC, Oakmont, PA
			Colin Montgomerie (78)	
1995	Corey Pavin	280	Greg Norman	Shinnecock Hills GC,
				Southampton, NY
1996	Steve Jones	278	Tom Lehman	Oakland Hills CC, Birmingham, MI
			Davis Love III	
1997	Ernie Els	276	Colin Montgomerie	Congressional CC, Bethesda, MD
1998	Lee Janzen	280	Payne Stewart	The Olympic Club, San Francisco, CA

Oldest champion *(years/months/days)*
    45/0/15 — Hale Irwin (1990)
Youngest champion
    19/10/14 — John J. McDermott (1911)
Most victories
    4 — Willie Anderson (1901, '03, '04, '05)
    4 — Robert T. Jones, Jr. (1923, '26, '29, '30)
    4 — Ben Hogan (1948, '50, '51, '53)
    4 — Jack Nicklaus (1962, '67, '72, '80)
    3 — Hale Irwin (1974, '79, '90)
    2 — by 13 players: Alex Smith (1906, '10),
        John J. McDermott (1911, '12), Walter
        Hagen (1914, '19), Gene Sarazen (1922,
        '32), Ralph Guldahl (1937, '38), Cary
        Middlecoff (1949, '56), Julius Boros (1952,
        '63), Billy Casper (1959, '66), Lee Trevino
        (1968, '71), Andy North (1978, '85), Curtis
        Strange (1988, '89), Ernie Els (1994, '97),
        and Lee Janzen (1993, '98).
Consecutive victories
    Willie Anderson (1903, '04, '05)
    John J. McDermott (1911, '12)
    Robert T. Jones, Jr. (1929, '30)
    Ralph Guldahl (1937, '38)
    Ben Hogan (1950, '51)
    Curtis Strange (1988, '89)
Most times runner-up
    4 — Sam Snead
    4 — Robert T. Jones, Jr.
    4 — Arnold Palmer
    4 — Jack Nicklaus
Longest course
    7,213 yards — Congressional CC, Bethesda,
        MD (1997)
Shortest course
    Since World War II
    6,528 yards — Merion GC (East Course),
        Ardmore, PA (1971, '81)
Most often host club of Open
    7 — Baltusrol GC, Springfield, NJ (1903, '15,
        '36, '54, '67, '80, '93)
    7 — Oakmont (PA) CC (1927, '35, '53, '62, '73,
        '83, '94)
Largest entry
    7,117 (1998)
Smallest entry
    11 (1895)
Lowest score, 72 holes
    272 — Jack Nicklaus (63-71-70-68), at Baltusrol
        GC (Lower Course), Springfield, NJ (1980)
    272 — Lee Janzen (67-67-69-69), at Baltusrol
        GC (Lower Course), Springfield, NJ (1993)
Lowest score, first 54 holes
    203 — George Burns (69-66-68), at Merion GC
        (East Course), Ardmore, PA (1981)

203 — Tze-Chung Chen (65-69-69), at Oakland
        Hills CC (South Course), Birmingham,
        MI (1985)
203 — Lee Janzen (67-67-69), at Baltusrol GC
        (Lower Course), Springfield, NJ (1993)
Lowest score, last 54 holes
    203 — Loren Roberts (69-64-70), at Oakmont
        CC, Oakmont, PA (1994)
Lowest score, first 36 holes
    134 — Jack Nicklaus (63-71), at Baltusrol GC
        (Lower Course), Springfield, NJ (1980)
    134 — Chen Tze-Chung (65-69), at Oakland Hills
        CC (South Course), Birmingham, MI (1985)
    134 — Lee Janzen (67-67), at Baltusrol GC
        (Lower Course), Springfield, NJ (1993)
Lowest score, last 36 holes
    132 — Larry Nelson (65-67), at Oakmont CC,
        Oakmont, PA (1983)
Lowest score, 9 holes
    29 — Neal Lancaster (second nine, fourth
        round) at Shinnecock Hills GC,
        Southampton, NY (1995)
    29 — Neal Lancaster (second nine, second
        round) at Oakland Hills CC, Birmingham,
        MI (1996)
Lowest score, 18 holes
    63 — Johnny Miller, fourth round at Oakmont
        CC, Oakmont, PA (1973)
    63 — Jack Nicklaus, first round at Baltusrol
        GC (Lower Course), Springfield, NJ (1980)
    63 — Tom Weiskopf, first round at Baltusrol
        GC (Lower Course), Springfield, NJ (1980)
Largest winning margin
    11 — Willie Smith (315), at Baltimore (MD)
        CC (Roland Park Course) (1899)
Highest winning score
    Since World War II
    293 — Julius Boros, at The Country Club,
        Brookline, MA (1963) (won in playoff)
Best start by champion
    63 — Jack Nicklaus, at Baltusrol GC (Lower
        Course), Springfield, NJ (1980)
Best finish by champion
    63 — Johnny Miller, at Oakmont (PA) CC (1973)
Worst start by champion
    Since World War II
    76 — Ben Hogan, at Oakland Hills CC (South
        Course), Birmingham, MI (1951)
    76 — Jack Fleck, at The Olympic Club (Lake
        Course), San Francisco, CA (1955)
Worst finish by champion
    Since World War II
    75 — Cary Middlecoff, at Medinah CC
        (No. 3 Course), Medinah, IL (1949)
    75 — Hale Irwin, at Inverness Club, Toledo,
        OH (1979)

Lowest score to lead field, 18 holes
> 63 — Jack Nicklaus and Tom Weiskopf, at Baltusrol GC (Lower Course), Springfield, NJ (1980)

Lowest score to lead field, 36 holes
> 134 — Jack Nicklaus (63-71), at Baltusrol GC (Lower Course), Springfield, NJ (1980)
> 134 — Chen Tze-Chung (65-69), at Oakland Hills CC (South Course), Birmingham, MI (1985)
> 134 — Lee Janzen (67-67), at Baltusrol GC (Lower Course), Springfield, NJ (1993)

Lowest score to lead field, 54 holes
> 203 — George Burns (69-66-68), at Merion GC (East Course), Ardmore, PA (1981)
> 203 — Chen Tze-Chung (65-69-69), at Oakland Hills CC (South Course), Birmingham, MI (1985)
> 203 — Lee Janzen (67-67-69), at Baltusrol GC (Lower Course), Springfield, NJ (1993)

Highest score to lead field, 18 holes
> *Since World War II*
> 71 — Sam Snead, at Oakland Hills CC (South Course), Birmingham, MI (1951)
> 71 — Tommy Bolt, Julius Boros, and Dick Metz, at Southern Hills CC, Tulsa, OK (1958)
> 71 — Tony Jacklin, at Hazeltine National GC, Chaska, MN (1970)
> 71 — Orville Moody, Jack Nicklaus, Chi Chi Rodriguez, Mason Rudolph, Tom Shaw, and Kermit Zarley, at Pebble Beach (CA) Golf Links (1972)

Highest score to lead field, 36 holes
> *Since World War II*
> 144 — Bobby Locke (73-71), at Oakland Hills CC (South Course), Birmingham, MI (1951)
> 144 — Tommy Bolt (67-77) and E. Harvie Ward (74-70), at The Olympic Club (Lake Course), San Francisco, CA (1955)
> 144 — Homero Blancas (74-70), Bruce Crampton (74-70), Jack Nicklaus (71-73), Cesar Seduno (72-72), Lanny Wadkins (76-68) and Kermit Zarley (71-73), at Pebble Beach (CA) Golf Links (1972)

Highest score to lead field, 54 holes
> *Since World War II*
> 218 — Bobby Locke (73-71-74), at Oakland Hills CC (South Course), Birmingham, MI (1951)
> 218 — Jacky Cupit (70-72-76), at The Country Club, Brookline, MA (1963)

Highest 36-hole cut
> 155 — at The Olympic Club (Lakeside Course), San Francisco, CA (1955)

Most players to tie for lead, 18 holes
> 7 — at Pebble Beach (CA) Golf Links (1972); at Southern Hills CC, Tulsa, OK (1977); and at Shinnecock Hills GC, Southampton, NY (1896)

Most players to tie for lead, 36 holes
> 6 — at Pebble Beach (CA) Golf Links (1972)

Most players to tie for lead, 54 holes
> 4 — at Oakmont (PA) CC (1973)

Most sub-par rounds, championship
> 124 — at Medinah CC (No. 3 Course), Medinah, IL (1990)

Most sub-par 72-hole totals, championship
> 28 — at Medinah CC (No. 3 Course), Medinah, IL (1990)

Most sub-par scores, first round
> 39 — at Medinah CC (No. 3 Course), Medinah, IL (1990)

Most sub-par scores, second round
> 47 — at Medinah CC (No. 3 Course), Medinah, IL (1990)

Most sub-par scores, third round
> 24 — at Medinah CC (No. 3 Course), Medinah, IL (1990)

Most sub-par scores, fourth round
> 18 — at Baltusrol GC (Lower Course), Springfield, NJ (1993)

Most sub-par rounds by one player in one championship
> 4 — Billy Casper, at The Olympic Club (Lakeside Course), San Francisco, CA (1966)
> 4 — Lee Trevino, at Oak Hill CC (East Course), Rochester, NY (1968)
> 4 — Tony Jacklin, at Hazeltine National GC, Chaska, MN (1970)
> 4 — Lee Janzen, at Baltusrol GC (Lower Course), Springfield, NJ (1993)

Highest score, one hole
> 19 — Ray Ainsley, at the 16th (par 4) at Cherry Hills CC, Englewood, CO (1938)

Most consecutive birdies
> 6 — George Burns (holes 2–7), at Pebble Beach (CA) Golf Links (1972) and Andy Dillard (holes 1-6), at Pebble Beach (CA) Golf Links (1992)

Most consecutive 3s
> 7 — Hubert Green (holes 10–16), at Southern Hills Country Club, Tulsa, OK (1977)
> 7 — Peter Jacobsen (holes 1–7), at The Country Club, Brookline, MA (1988)

Most consecutive Opens
> 42 — Jack Nicklaus (1957-98)

Most Opens completed 72 holes
> 35 — Jack Nicklaus

Most consecutive Opens completed 72 holes
> 22 — Walter Hagen (1913-36; no Championships 1917-18)
> 22 — Gene Sarazen (1920-41)
> 22 — Gary Player (1958-79)

Robert Sommers is the former editor and publisher of the USGA's *Golf Journal*, author of *The U.S. Open: Golf's Ultimate Challenge* and *Golf Anecdotes*, and is based in Port St. Lucie, Fla.

Michael Cohen is a photographer based in New York City and a contributor to many magazines and books.

Fred Vuich is a staff photographer for *Golf Magazine*, a contributor to many books, and is based in Pittsburgh.